WELCOME TO THE U.S.A.
CALIFORNIA

Written by Ann Heinrichs   Illustrated by Matt Kania
Content Adviser: Dr. Eileen Keremitsis, Historian
and Author, San Francisco, California

The Child's World

Published in the United States of America by The Child's World®
PO Box 326 • Chanhassen, MN 55317-0326
800-599-READ • www.childsworld.com

Photo Credits

Cover: Photodisc; frontispiece: Photodisc.

Interior: Californians for Schwarzenegger: 15; Charles Schulz Museum, Santa Rosa, CA: 30, 31 (Brian Lankers); Corbis: 6 (C. Moore), 33 (Neil Rabinowitz); Getty Images: 14 (AFP/Robyn Beck), 21 (The Image Bank/Darrell Gulin); Getty Images/Stone: 29 (Darrell Gulin), 34 (Lawrence Migdale); Jim Graves/Mission San Juan Capistrano: 9; Robert Holmes/California Tourism: 13; Intel Museum: 18; Catherine Karnow/Corbis: 25, 26; NASA/JPL: 17; Sara M. Skinner/Petaluma Adobe State Historic Park: 10; SeaWorld San Diego: 22.

Acknowledgments

The Child's World®: Mary Berendes, Publishing Director

Editorial Directions, Inc.: E. Russell Primm, Editorial Director; Katie Marsico, Associate Editor; Judith Shiffer, Assistant Editor; Matt Messbarger, Editorial Assistant; Susan Hindman, Copy Editor; Melissa McDaniel, Proofreader; Peter Garnham, Matt Messbarger, Olivia Nellums, Chris Simms, Molly Symmonds, Katherine Trickle, Carl Stephen Wender, Fact Checkers; Tim Griffin/IndexServ, Indexer; Cian Loughlin O'Day, Photo Researcher and Editor

The Design Lab: Kathleen Petelinsek, Design and Art Direction; Kari Thornborough, Page Production

Library of Congress Cataloging-in-Publication Data

Heinrichs, Ann.
  California / written by Ann Heinrichs ; cartography and illustrations by Matt Kania.
     p. cm. — (Welcome to the U.S.A.)
  Includes index.
  ISBN 1-59296-283-1 (lib. bdg. : alk. paper)
  1. California—Juvenile literature. 2. California—Geography—Juvenile literature.
  I. Kania, Matt. II. Title. III. Series.
  F861.3.H45 2004
  979.4—dc22   2004005704

Ann Heinrichs is the author of more than 100 books for children and young adults. She has also enjoyed successful careers as a children's book editor and an advertising copywriter. Ann grew up in Fort Smith, Arkansas, and lives in Chicago, Illinois.

**About the Author
Ann Heinrichs**

Matt Kania loves maps and, as a kid, dreamed of making them. In school he studied geography and cartography, and today he makes maps for a living. Matt's favorite thing about drawing maps is learning about the places they represent. Many of the maps he has created can be found in books, magazines, videos, Web sites, and public places.

**About the
Map Illustrator
Matt Kania**

On the cover: The Golden Gate Bridge is beautiful at night.
On page one: Those Joshua trees look spooky at sunset!

OUR CALIFORNIA TRIP

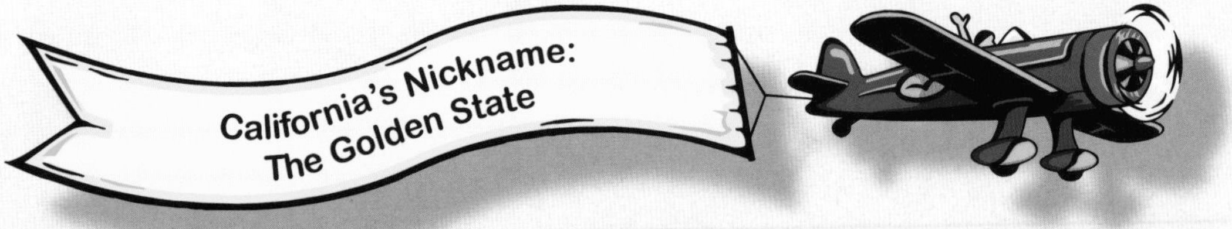
California's Nickname:
The Golden State

Hey—let's check out the Golden State! Just follow the dotted line, or else skip around. Either way, you're in for a great ride. You'll meet Walt Disney, Arnold Schwarzenegger, and Charles Schulz. You'll visit gold mines, tar pits, and space labs. So buckle up that seat belt. We're on our way!

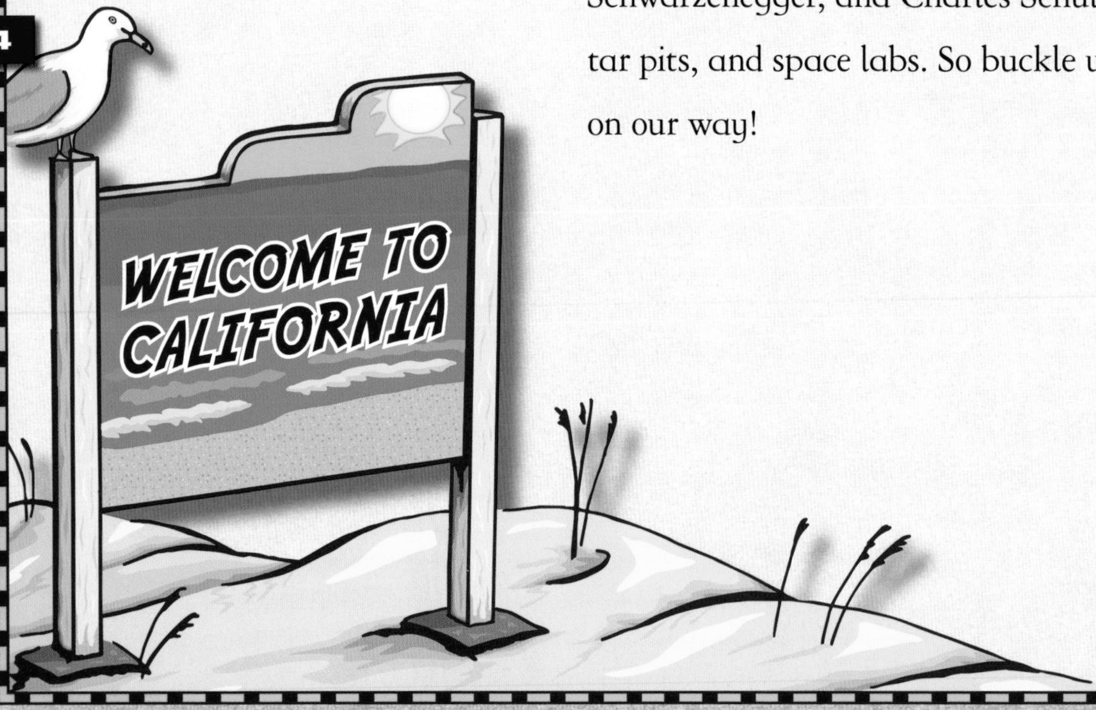
WELCOME TO
CALIFORNIA

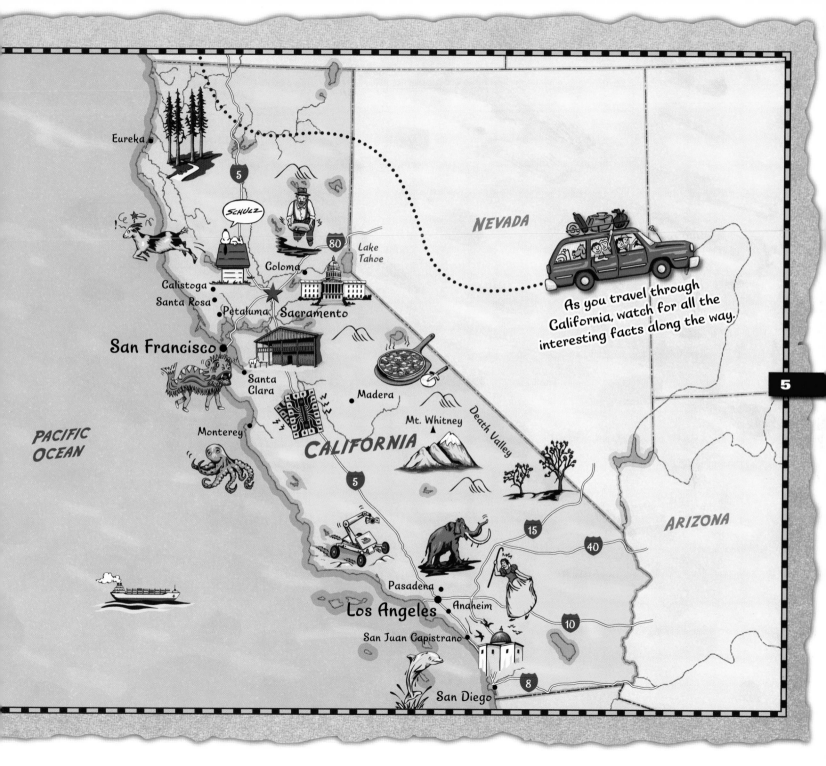

As you travel through California, watch for all the interesting facts along the way.

Help! Will our feet get stuck? Will we sink into the black, sticky goo?

Y ou'll find La Brea Tar Pits in Los Angeles. It was a weird scene thousands of years ago. Tar bubbled up from deep underground. It formed pools of black, sticky goo.

Thousands of animals got stuck in the tar. Later, scientists began finding their bones. They found wolves, bears, and mammoths. They even found lions, camels, and saber-toothed cats.

The tar was useful to Native Americans. They used it as a glue. They also used it in making canoes and baskets. The tar made a tight seal. It kept water from seeping in.

A mammoth is stuck in La Brea tar! Models show the animals that died there long ago.

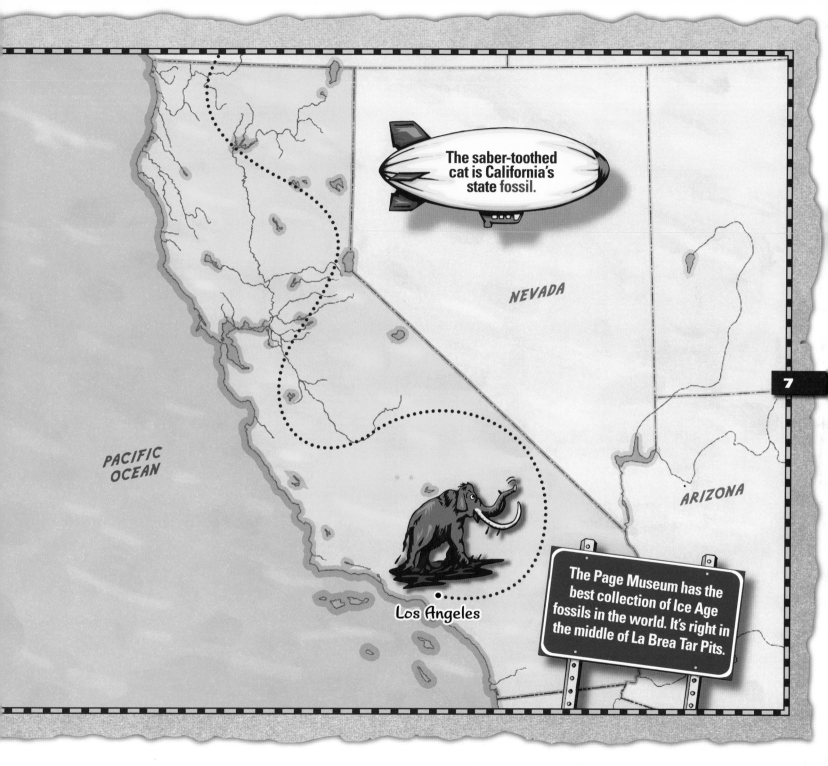

The saber-toothed cat is California's state fossil.

NEVADA

ARIZONA

PACIFIC OCEAN

Los Angeles

The Page Museum has the best collection of Ice Age fossils in the world. It's right in the middle of La Brea Tar Pits.

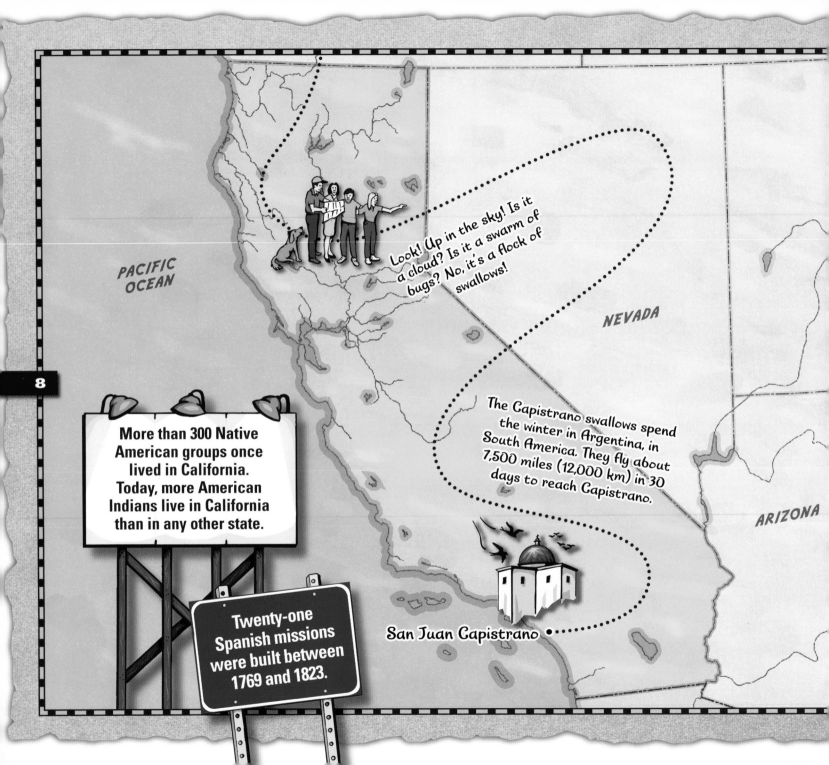

PACIFIC OCEAN

NEVADA

ARIZONA

Look! Up in the sky! Is it a cloud? Is it a swarm of bugs? No, it's a flock of swallows!

The Capistrano swallows spend the winter in Argentina, in South America. They fly about 7,500 miles (12,000 km) in 30 days to reach Capistrano.

More than 300 Native American groups once lived in California. Today, more American Indians live in California than in any other state.

Twenty-one Spanish missions were built between 1769 and 1823.

San Juan Capistrano

The Swallows at San Juan Capistrano

San Juan Capistrano is famous for its swallows. These little birds fly in every March to nest there. Thousands of people come to see them.

San Juan Capistrano is one of the California **Missions.** They were the first European settlements in California. Spain ruled Mexico and California in the 1700s. Spanish people from Mexico moved into California. They built missions, forts, and villages. All these Spanish settlements became California cities.

Father Junípero Serra was a Catholic priest, or padre. He came from Mexico to build missions. He taught Christianity to the American Indians. Father Serra founded Mission San Juan Capistrano in 1776.

Swallow Day is March 19. These children are dressed up as padres.

Who Lived Here before Europeans Arrived? Hupa, Maidu, Modoc, Mojave, and Pomo

Baa! Is it time for a haircut at Petaluma Adobe?

Can you shear a sheep? Here's how. First you grab the sheep. Then you start shaving it. So what's the hard part? Removing all the wool in one big piece!

Want to watch an expert do it? Just go to Sheep Shearing Day at Petaluma Adobe. That's when the sheep get their haircuts.

Petaluma Adobe was California's biggest ranch house. Hundreds of ranches covered California in the 1800s. How did the ranches begin? Mexico won freedom from Spain in 1821. Then Mexico ruled California. Mexico gave away most of the missions' land. It was divided into huge pieces of land called ranchos. The landowners were called rancheros. They grew rich raising cattle and sheep.

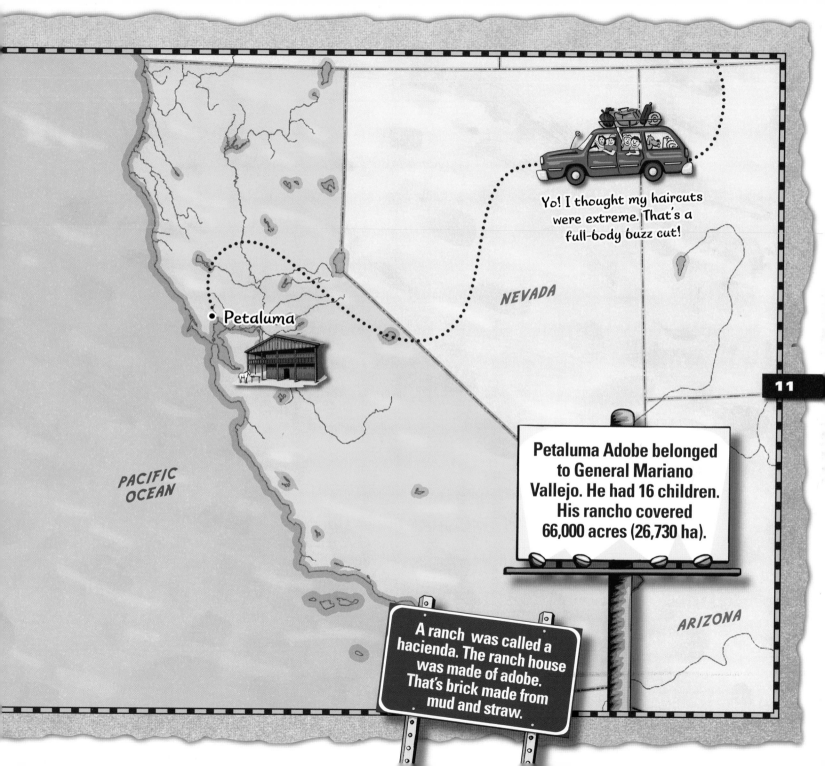

Yo! I thought my haircuts were extreme. That's a full-body buzz cut!

NEVADA

• Petaluma

PACIFIC OCEAN

ARIZONA

Petaluma Adobe belonged to General Mariano Vallejo. He had 16 children. His rancho covered 66,000 acres (26,730 ha).

A ranch was called a hacienda. The ranch house was made of adobe. That's brick made from mud and straw.

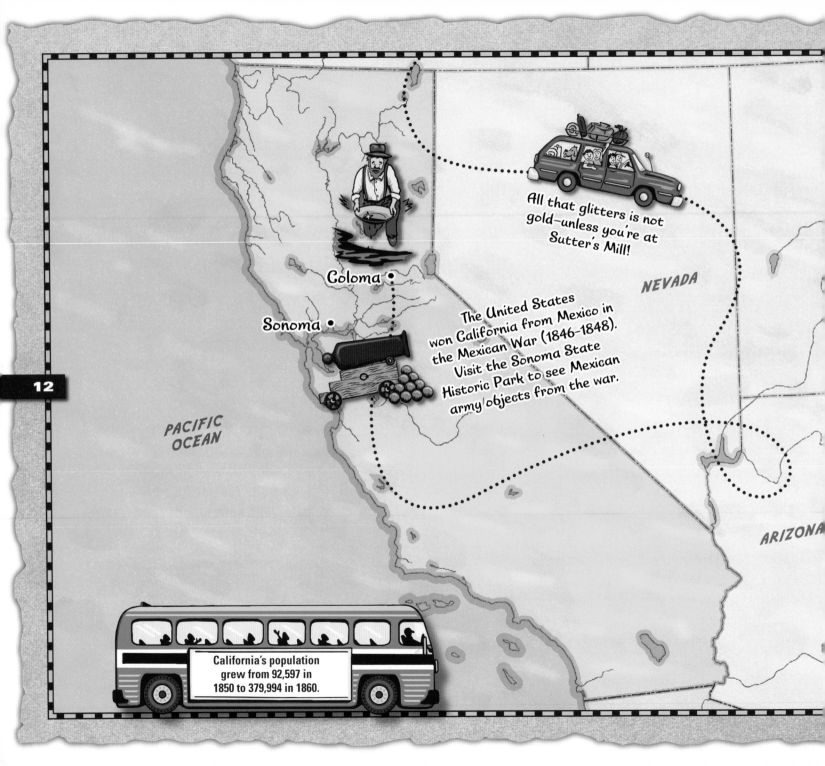

All that glitters is not gold—unless you're at Sutter's Mill!

NEVADA

Coloma •

Sonoma •

The United States won California from Mexico in the Mexican War (1846–1848). Visit the Sonoma State Historic Park to see Mexican army objects from the war.

PACIFIC OCEAN

ARIZONA

California's population grew from 92,597 in 1850 to 379,994 in 1860.

Panning for Gold at Sutter's Mill

Want to find some gold? Just go to Sutter's Mill in Coloma. You can get a big old pan there. Then go down by the American River. Let the water flow into your pan. Do you see something sparkly? It's gold!

That's what John Marshall did in 1848. He was building a sawmill by the American River. One day he found gold in the river. His gold discovery started the California gold rush. By 1849, thousands of people were pouring in. They were called Forty-Niners. You can probably guess why!

New towns sprang up overnight. But people left if they didn't find gold. Some towns became ghost towns.

In 1849, miners headed west for Sutter's Mill. They were looking for gold.

California was the 31st state to enter the Union. It joined on September 9, 1850.

13

It's here, it's there, it's everywhere. It's that big ol' grizzly bear.

The Bear Flag and the State Capitol

The bear flag is California's state flag. The first bear flag showed up in 1846. American settlers in Sonoma made it. Now bear flags are everywhere in California. Just walk around inside the state capitol. They're hanging all over the place!

Many state government offices are in the capitol. California has three branches of government. One branch makes laws. Its members come from all over the state. The governor heads another branch. It carries out the laws. Courts make up the third branch. They decide whether someone has broken the law.

Are you looking for Arnold Schwarzenegger? Search the state capitol in Sacramento.

Welcome to Sacramento, the capital of California!

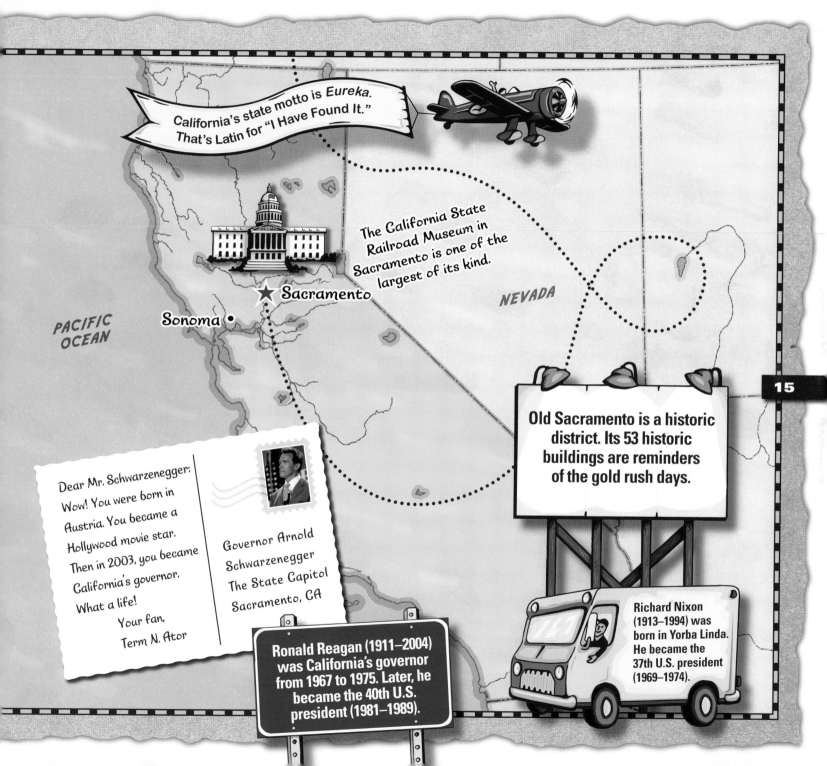

California's state motto is *Eureka.*
That's Latin for "I Have Found It."

The California State Railroad Museum in Sacramento is one of the largest of its kind.

NEVADA

★ Sacramento

Sonoma •

PACIFIC OCEAN

Old Sacramento is a historic district. Its 53 historic buildings are reminders of the gold rush days.

Dear Mr. Schwarzenegger:
Wow! You were born in Austria. You became a Hollywood movie star. Then in 2003, you became California's governor. What a life!
Your fan,
Term N. Ator

Governor Arnold Schwarzenegger
The State Capitol
Sacramento, CA

Richard Nixon (1913–1994) was born in Yorba Linda. He became the 37th U.S. president (1969–1974).

Ronald Reagan (1911–2004) was California's governor from 1967 to 1975. Later, he became the 40th U.S. president (1981–1989).

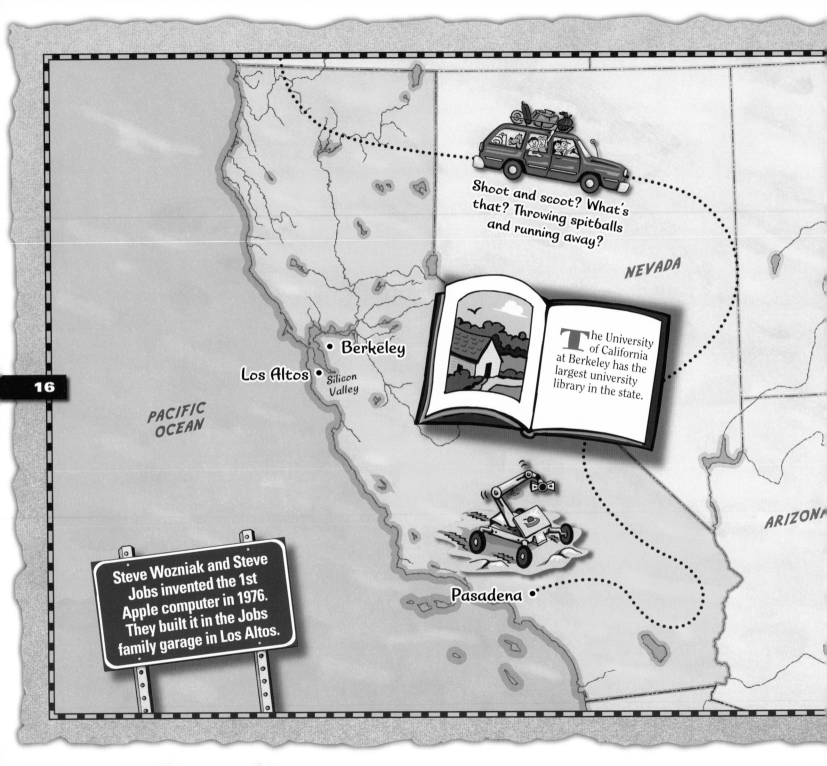

Shoot and scoot? What's that? Throwing spitballs and running away?

NEVADA

• Berkeley

Los Altos • Silicon Valley

The University of California at Berkeley has the largest university library in the state.

PACIFIC OCEAN

ARIZONA

Pasadena •

Steve Wozniak and Steve Jobs invented the 1st Apple computer in 1976. They built it in the Jobs family garage in Los Altos.

Maybe you'll become an astronaut who explores space. Check out Pasadena's Jet Propulsion Lab.

What do Mars **rovers** do? They "shoot and scoot"! They take pictures and then they scoot somewhere else. Just tour the Jet Propulsion Laboratory in Pasadena. It makes **robot** spacecraft. You'll see how scientists make those rovers scoot!

Space science is a big **industry** in California. America's space program did lots of testing there. Computer science became another hot industry. Many computer companies grew up in the Santa Clara Valley. Now that area is called Silicon Valley. Silicon is a material used in making **computer chips.**

If you weigh 50 pounds (23 kg) on Earth, you'd weigh less than 19 pounds (9 kg) on Mars.

The Intel Museum in Santa Clara

The Intel Museum is a fun place to visit. It's in Santa Clara. That's right in the heart of Silicon Valley.

Intel is the world's largest maker of computer chips. Its factory workers wear outfits called bunny suits! The suits keep the tiny computer parts clean. They keep people's hairs and skin flakes away. Kids love to visit Intel's museum. They get to try on bunny suits, too.

California makes more products than any other state. Computers and **electronics** are its major factory goods. Most are made in Silicon Valley. Foods are important factory products, too.

Do you like computers? Then don't forget to visit the Intel Museum!

Frank Epperson of San Francisco invented the popsicle in 1905. He was just 11 then!

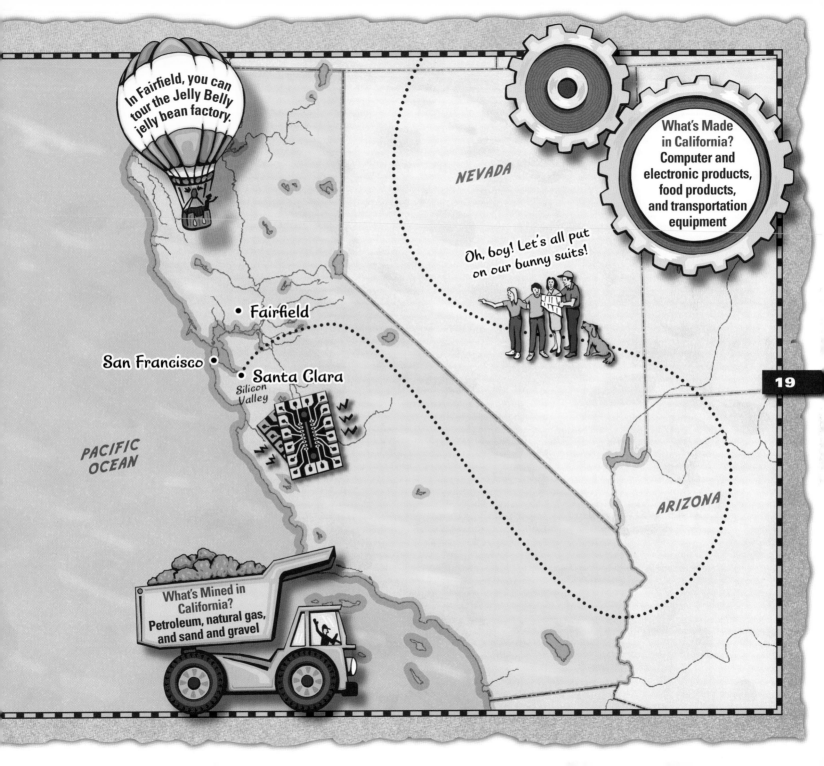

In Fairfield, you can tour the Jelly Belly jelly bean factory.

NEVADA

What's Made in California? Computer and electronic products, food products, and transportation equipment

Oh, boy! Let's all put on our bunny suits!

Fairfield

San Francisco

Santa Clara

Silicon Valley

PACIFIC OCEAN

ARIZONA

What's Mined in California? Petroleum, natural gas, and sand and gravel

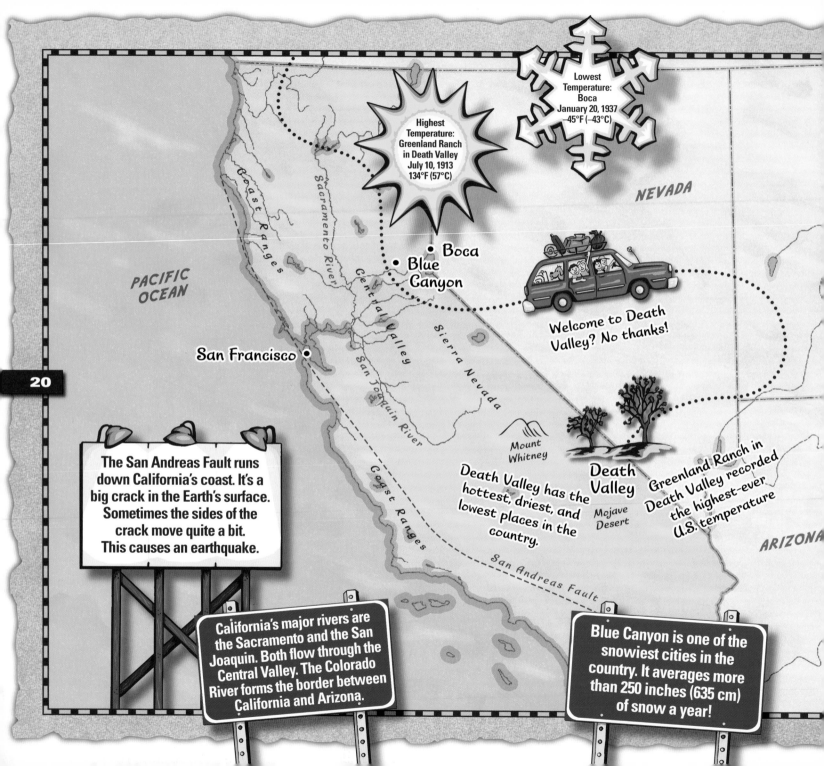

Highest Temperature: Greenland Ranch in Death Valley July 10, 1913 134°F (57°C)

Lowest Temperature: Boca January 20, 1937 –45°F (–43°C)

NEVADA

Boca

Blue Canyon

PACIFIC OCEAN

San Francisco

Coast Ranges

Sacramento River

Central Valley

Sierra Nevada

San Joaquin River

Mount Whitney

Welcome to Death Valley? No thanks!

Death Valley

Mojave Desert

Death Valley has the hottest, driest, and lowest places in the country.

Greenland Ranch in Death Valley recorded the highest-ever U.S. temperature

Coast Ranges

San Andreas Fault

ARIZONA

The San Andreas Fault runs down California's coast. It's a big crack in the Earth's surface. Sometimes the sides of the crack move quite a bit. This causes an earthquake.

California's major rivers are the Sacramento and the San Joaquin. Both flow through the Central Valley. The Colorado River forms the border between California and Arizona.

Blue Canyon is one of the snowiest cities in the country. It averages more than 250 inches (635 cm) of snow a year!

Death Valley, Deserts, and Coasts

Death Valley has a pretty scary name. But it's not all that deadly. Lots of animals and plants live there. If they can stand it, you can!

Southeastern California is mostly deserts. One of them is Death Valley. Another is the Mojave Desert. Western California is much wetter. It faces the Pacific Ocean. The northern coast is often foggy and rainy. The southern coast is warm and sunny.

Two big mountain ranges run down California. The Coast Ranges rise near the coast. The Sierra Nevada is in eastern California. Between them is the Central Valley. It's a rich farming region.

Can you imagine living in a hot desert? Coyotes and other animals live in Death Valley.

California gets lots of earthquakes. San Francisco had a terrible earthquake in 1906.

HIGHEST AND LOWEST POINTS
Highest: Mount Whitney at 14,495 feet (4,418 m)
Lowest: 282 feet (86 m) below sea level in Death Valley

San Diego's SeaWorld

Eew! This one's slick and slippery. Ouch! This one's pointy. What are they? A bat ray and a starfish. You can touch them at San Diego's SeaWorld.

Plenty of sea critters live off California's coast. Crabs, lobsters, and dolphins are just a few. Foxes, jackrabbits, and mice live in the deserts. They scurry around cactuses and other tough plants. Bighorn sheep prance up in the mountains. You'll be lucky to see them, though. They're very shy!

Chomp! Sharks have sharp teeth. Luckily, you can watch them in safety at SeaWorld.

The Frog Tunnel is at Toad Hollow in Davis. It was built so frogs could safely cross the road.

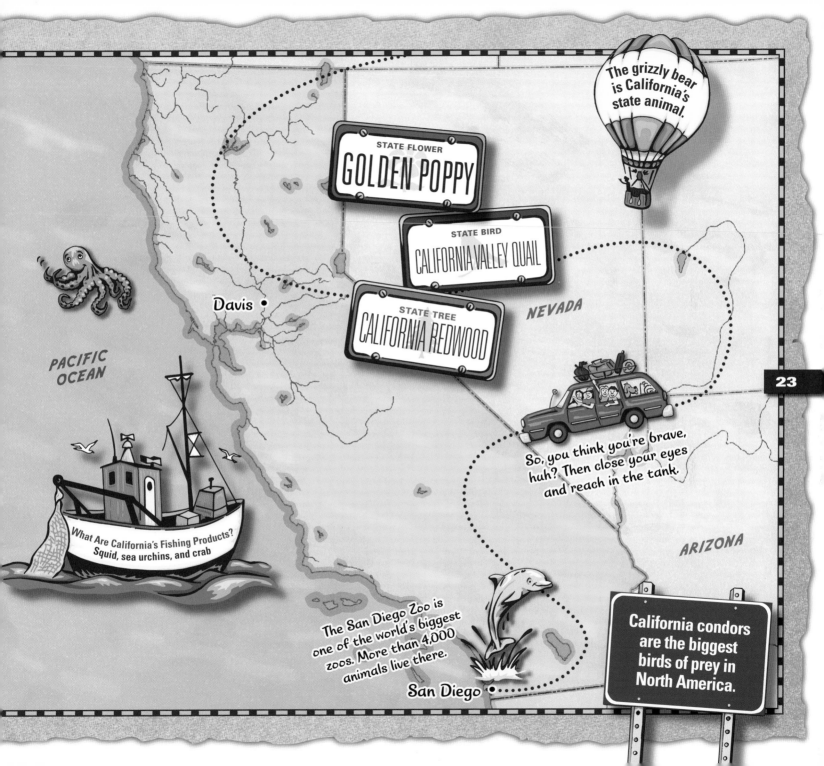

The grizzly bear is California's state animal.

STATE FLOWER
GOLDEN POPPY

STATE BIRD
CALIFORNIA VALLEY QUAIL

STATE TREE
CALIFORNIA REDWOOD

NEVADA

Davis •

PACIFIC OCEAN

So, you think you're brave, huh? Then close your eyes and reach in the tank.

ARIZONA

What Are California's Fishing Products?
Squid, sea urchins, and crab

The San Diego Zoo is one of the world's biggest zoos. More than 4,000 animals live there.

San Diego •

California condors are the biggest birds of prey in North America.

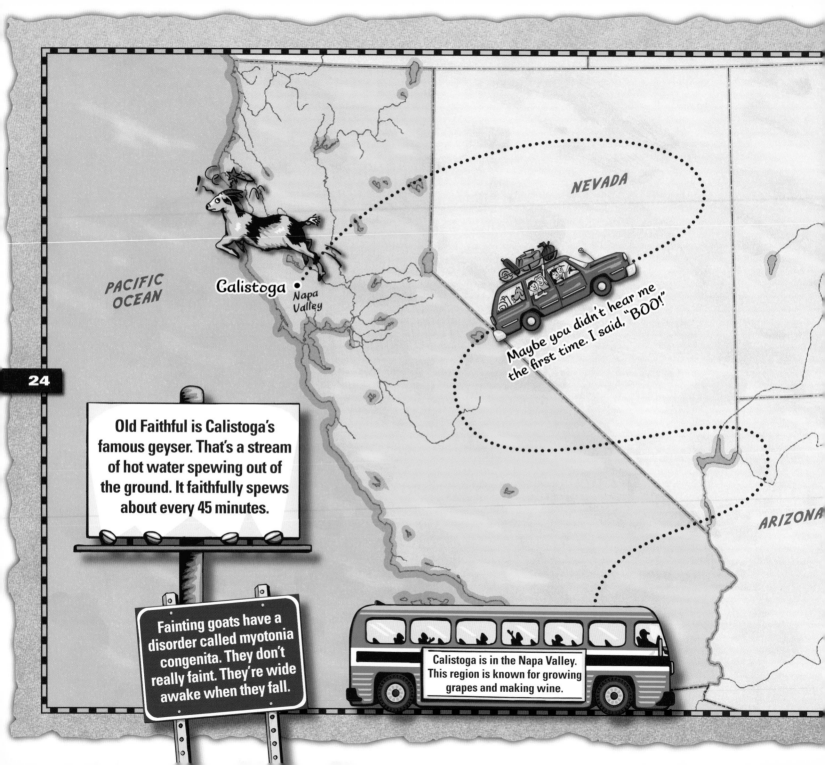

NEVADA

PACIFIC
OCEAN

Calistoga •
Napa
Valley

ARIZONA

Maybe you didn't hear me
the first time, I said, "BOO!"

Old Faithful is Calistoga's
famous geyser. That's a stream
of hot water spewing out of
the ground. It faithfully spews
about every 45 minutes.

Fainting goats have a
disorder called myotonia
congenita. They don't
really faint. They're wide
awake when they fall.

Calistoga is in the Napa Valley.
This region is known for growing
grapes and making wine.

Calistoga and the Fainting Goats

Boo! That's all it takes. Kerplunk! The goat's on the ground. It's stiff as a board. It must be a fainting goat!

Some California farmers raise fainting goats. Surprise one, and it gets stiff and falls over. Tourists come to see the fainting goats of Calistoga. But it takes a lot to scare them now. They're bored with people saying "Boo!"

There's a lot to Calistoga besides fainting goats!

Calistoga is best known for its hot-water springs. The water comes from deep underground.

The Giant Redwoods

Want to see the oldest, tallest trees around? Take a drive down the Avenue of the Giants.

You're driving along the Avenue of the Giants. It runs near California's north coast, near Eureka. You take a turn into the forest. All of a sudden, you're in a dark tunnel. You're driving right through a giant tree trunk!

California's redwood trees are huge. They are the world's tallest living things. People have cut tunnels through some redwoods' trunks. The result? Drive-through trees!

Redwoods once grew in the **Petrified** Forest, too. They lived more than three million years ago. Now they have turned to stone!

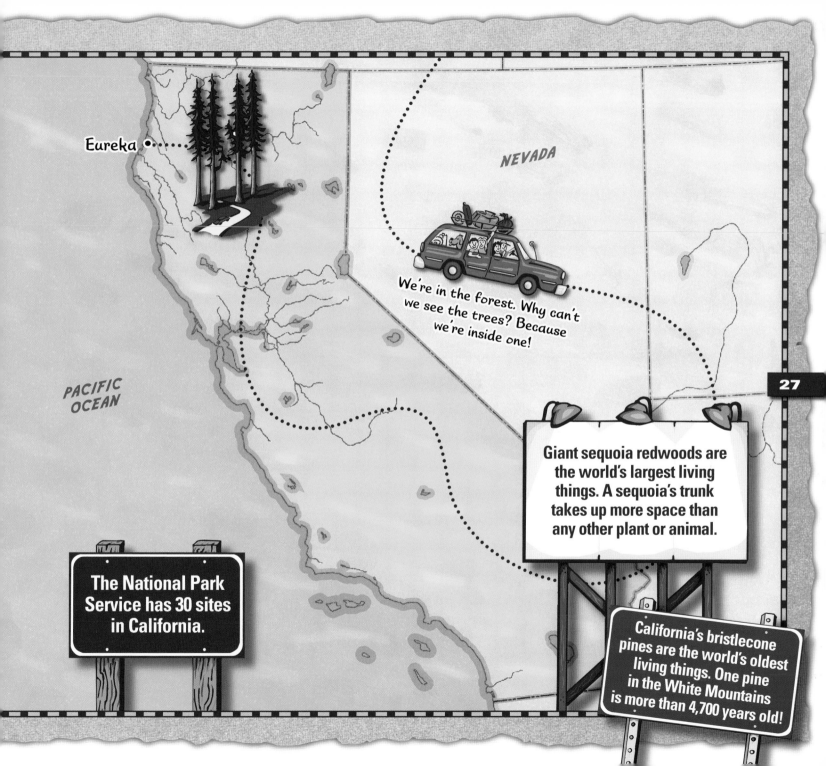

Eureka

NEVADA

PACIFIC
OCEAN

We're in the forest. Why can't we see the trees? Because we're inside one!

Giant sequoia redwoods are the world's largest living things. A sequoia's trunk takes up more space than any other plant or animal.

The National Park Service has 30 sites in California.

California's bristlecone pines are the world's oldest living things. One pine in the White Mountains is more than 4,700 years old!

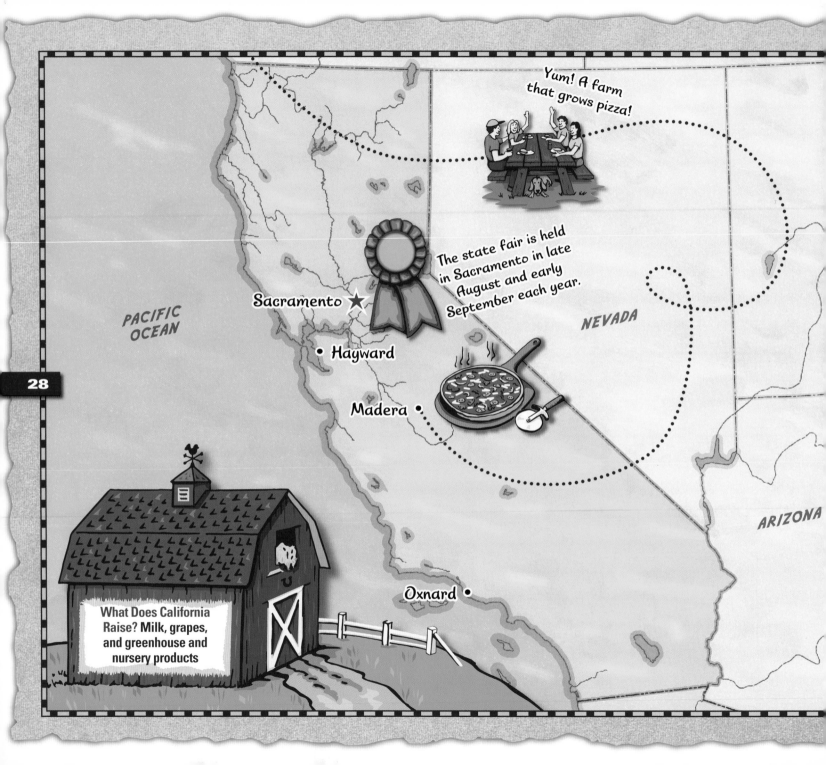

Madera's Pizza Farm

Be sure and drink your milk! California farmers raise both beef and dairy cattle.

Check out the Pizza Farm in Madera. It grows all the things that go into pizza. The farm is even shaped like a pizza! Each "slice" grows a different ingredient. There's wheat for the crust. There's dairy cattle for the cheese. There's tomatoes, peppers, and herbs. Is your mouth watering yet?

California is the nation's leading farm state. Some of the biggest farms are in the Central Valley. That's where the Pizza Farm is. The Imperial Valley in the south has lots of farms, too.

Fruits, nuts, and vegetables are important crops. Many farmers raise milk and beef cattle. Some raise sheep or chickens, too.

Ever had a strawberry pizza? You can get one at the Strawberry Festival in Oxnard.

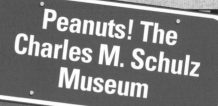

Santa Rosa had a famous resident— Charles M. Schulz. Schulz created the *Peanuts* comic strip. He thought up Snoopy, Charlie Brown, and Lucy. He invented Schroeder, Linus, and Peppermint Patty, too. Do you have a favorite *Peanuts* character?

The Charles M. Schulz Museum is fun to visit. It's full of *Peanuts* art. It also has a nice, cozy theater. There you can curl up and watch *Peanuts* cartoons. They run for hours!

Who's your favorite Peanuts character? Visit them all at the Charles M. Schulz Museum.

Wow! Hours and hours of cartoons! And nobody's going to send us to bed!

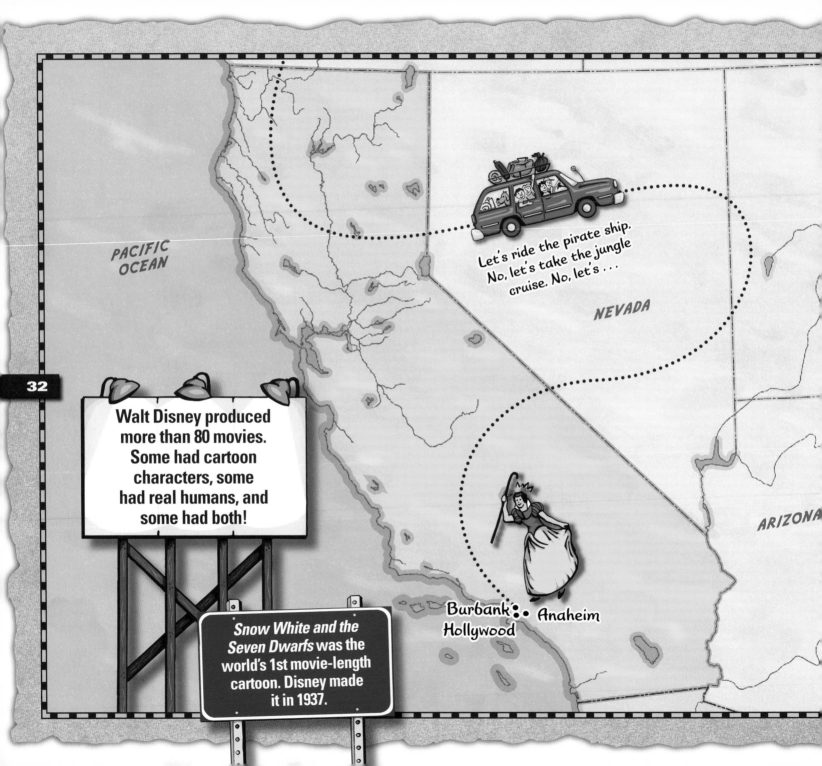

PACIFIC
OCEAN

Let's ride the pirate ship.
No, let's take the jungle
cruise. No, let's ...

NEVADA

ARIZONA

Walt Disney produced
more than 80 movies.
Some had cartoon
characters, some
had real humans, and
some had both!

*Snow White and the
Seven Dwarfs* was the
world's 1st movie-length
cartoon. Disney made
it in 1937.

Burbank •• Anaheim
Hollywood

Welcome to Disneyland!

Blast into space. Sail down a jungle river. Visit a fairy castle. Meet pirates, ghosts, and flying elephants. It could only happen in Disneyland!

Walt Disney invented Mickey Mouse in 1928. He made hundreds of cartoons and movies. But he wanted to create even more fun for kids. So he opened Disneyland in Anaheim.

Anaheim is close to Hollywood. That's the moviemaking capital of the world. Lots of television shows are made there, too.

Would you like to fly on an elephant? You can at Disneyland.

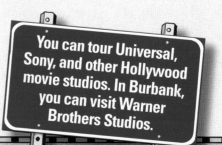

You can tour Universal, Sony, and other Hollywood movie studios. In Burbank, you can visit Warner Brothers Studios.

Do you see a dragon dancing in the street? Don't worry—it's just San Francisco's Chinese New Year.

Chinese New Year in San Francisco

Firecrackers are popping! Dragons are dancing down the street! It's Chinese New Year in San Francisco!

Many Chinese **immigrants** settled in San Francisco. They built up the Chinatown area. It's one of the biggest Chinese neighborhoods outside of Asia.

Many Hispanic, or Latino, people also live in California. Most have Mexican roots. Hispanic festivals are colorful and exciting. One is the Old Spanish Days Fiesta in Santa Barbara.

Dozens of other **ethnic** groups live in California. Each group has its special foods and customs. Want to see the world? Just visit California!

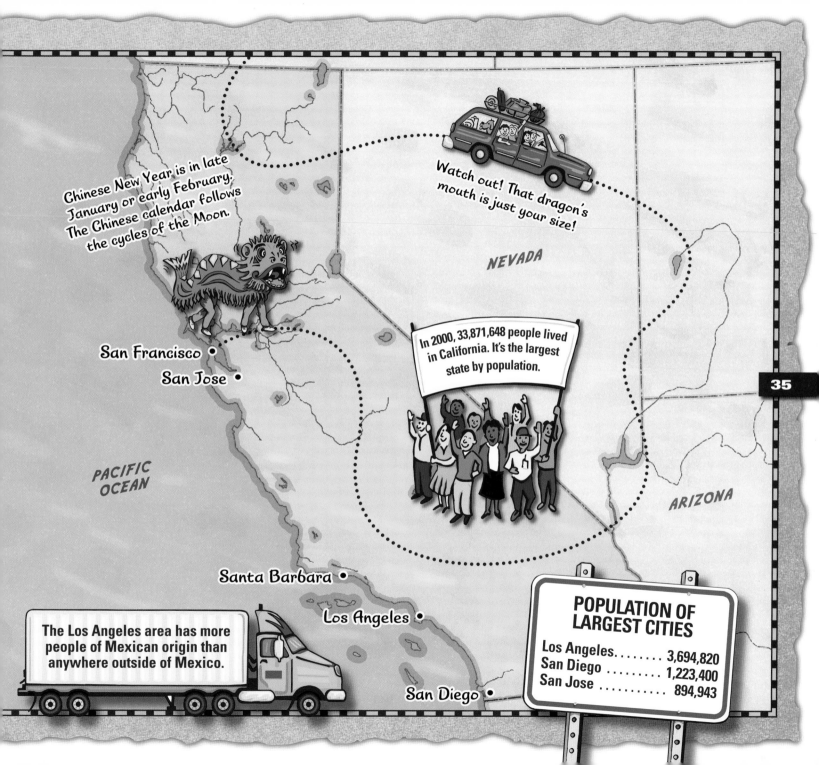

Chinese New Year is in late January or early February. The Chinese calendar follows the cycles of the Moon.

Watch out! That dragon's mouth is just your size!

NEVADA

In 2000, 33,871,648 people lived in California. It's the largest state by population.

San Francisco •
San Jose •

PACIFIC OCEAN

ARIZONA

Santa Barbara •

Los Angeles •

The Los Angeles area has more people of Mexican origin than anywhere outside of Mexico.

San Diego •

POPULATION OF LARGEST CITIES

Los Angeles........ 3,694,820
San Diego 1,223,400
San Jose 894,943

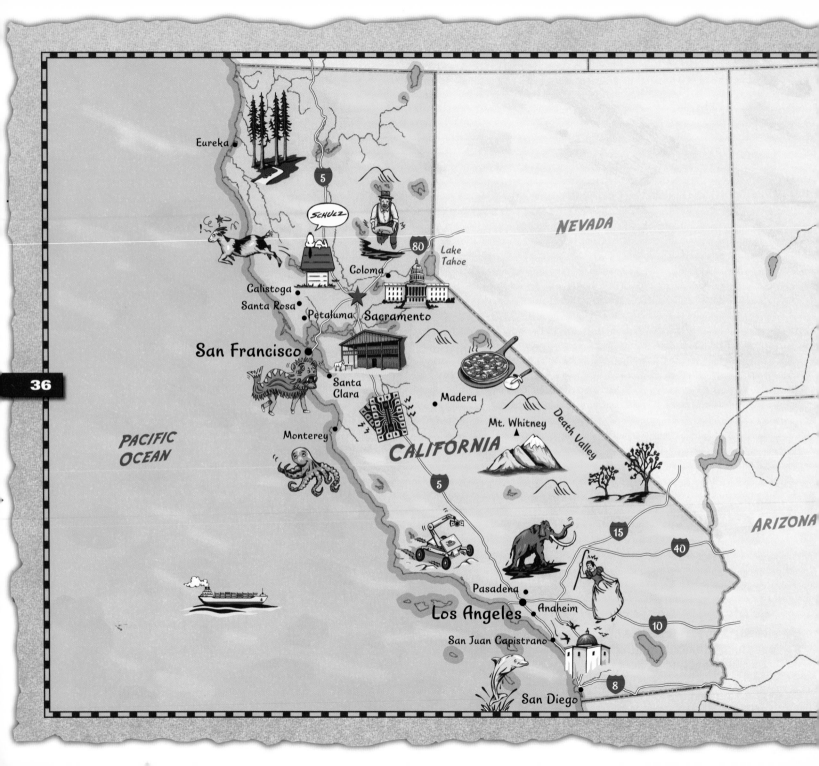

OUR TRIP

We visited many amazing places on our trip! We also met a lot of interesting people along the way. Look at the map on the left. Use your finger to trace all the places we have been.

Do you remember what California's state fossil is? See page 7 for the answer.

How many children did General Mariano Vallejo have? Page 11 has the answer.

Which U.S. president was born in California? See page 15 for the answer.

What tasty candies can you sample in Fairfield? Look on page 19 for the answer.

How many animals live at the San Diego Zoo? Page 23 has the answer.

Where can you get a strawberry pizza? Turn to page 29 for the answer.

What kind of drawing pen did Charles Schulz have? Look on page 31 and find out!

How many movies did Walt Disney produce? Turn to page 32 for the answer.

That was a great trip! We have traveled all over California!

There were a few places that we didn't have time for, though. Next time, we plan to visit the Monterey Bay Aquarium. There are about 550 different types of plants and animals on display! That number includes penguins, otters, sharks, turtles, and whales.

More Places to Visit in California

WORDS TO KNOW

computer chips (kuhm-PYOO-tur CHIPS) very small computer parts that make the computer work

electronics (i-lek-TRON-iks) a science that deals with tiny particles called electrons

ethnic (ETH-nik) relating to a person's race or nation

fossil (FOSS-uhl) a bone or print of something that lived on Earth long ago

immigrants (IM-uh-gruhnts) people who move from their home country to another country

industry (IN-duh-stree) a type of business

missions (MISH-uhnz) religious centers devoted to spreading a faith

petrified (PET-ruh-fide) turned into stone

robot (ROH-bot) a machine that can do human tasks

rovers (ROH-vurz) people or things that shift from place to place

California covers 155,959 square miles (403,933 sq km). It's the 3rd-largest state in size.

STATE SYMBOLS

State animal: California grizzly bear

State bird: California valley quail

State fish: Golden trout

State flower: California poppy (golden poppy)

State fossil: Saber-toothed cat

State gemstone: Blue diamond (benitoite)

State insect: California dogface butterfly

State marine fish: Garibaldi

State marine mammal: California gray whale

State mineral: Gold

State reptile: Desert tortoise

State rock: Serpentine

State soil: San Joaquin soil

State tree: California redwood

State flag

State seal

STATE SONG

"I Love You, California"
Words by F. B. Silverwood, music by A. F. Frankenstein

I love you, California, you're the greatest state of all.
I love you in the winter, summer, spring and in the fall.
I love your fertile valleys, your dear mountains I adore.
I love your grand old ocean and I love her rugged shore.

Chorus:
Where the snow-crowned Golden Sierras
Keep their watch o'er the valleys' bloom,
It is there I would be in our land by the sea,
Ev'ry breeze bearing rich perfume.
It is here nature gives of her rarest. It is Home Sweet Home to me,
And I know when I die I shall breathe my last sigh
For my sunny California.

I love your redwood forests–love your fields of yellow grain.
I love your summer breezes and I love your winter rain.
I love you, land of flowers; land of honey, fruit and wine.
I love you, California; you have won this heart of mine.

I love your old gray Missions, love your vineyards stretching far.
I love you, California, with your Golden Gate ajar.
I love your purple sunsets, love your skies of azure blue.
I love you, California; I just can't help loving you.

I love you, Catalina, you are very dear to me;
I love you, Tamalpais, and I love Yosemite;
I love you, land of sunshine, half your beauties are untold;
I loved you in my childhood, and I'll love you when I'm old.

FAMOUS PEOPLE

Chávez, César (1927–1993), labor leader

Child, Julia (1912–2004), world-famous chef

Cleary, Beverly (1916–), children's author

DiMaggio, Joe (1914–1999), baseball legend

Disney, Walt (1901–1966), film producer, animator

Garcia, Jerry (1942–1995), singer with the Grateful Dead

Ishi (ca. 1862–1916), the last of the Yahi people

Johnson, Earvin "Magic" (1959–), basketball player

Johnson, Jimmie (1975–), NASCAR racer

Lucas, George (1944–), film director and producer

Marshall, James (1810–1885), gold miner

McGwire, Mark (1963–) baseball player

Monroe, Marilyn (1926–1962), movie star

Nixon, Richard (1913–1994), 37th U.S. president

Reagan, Ronald (1911–2004), 40th U.S. president

Ride, Sally K. (1951–), 1st American woman astronaut

Ryan, Pam Muñoz (1951–), children's author

Say, Allen (1937–), children's author

Schwarzenegger, Arnold (1947–), movie star and governor of California

Woods, Eldrick "Tiger" (1975–), champion golfer

Valens, Ritchie (1941–1959), legendary rock 'n' roll singer

TO FIND OUT MORE

At the Library
Bowler, Sarah. *Father Junípero Serra and the California Missions*. Chanhassen, Minn.: The Child's World, 2003.

Domeniconi, David, and Pam Carroll (illustrator). *G Is for Golden: A California Alphabet*. Chelsea, Mich.: Sleeping Bear Press, 2002.

Roop, Connie, and Peter Roop. *California Gold Rush*. New York: Scholastic Reference, 2002.

On the Web
Visit our home page for lots of links about California:
http://www.childsworld.com/links

Note to Parents, Teachers, and Librarians: We routinely verify our Web links to make sure they are safe, active sites—so encourage your readers to check them out!

Places to Visit or Contact
California Division of Tourism
801 K Street, Suite 1600
Sacramento, CA 95814
916/444-4429
For more information about traveling in California

California Historical Society
678 Mission Street
San Francisco, CA 94105
415/357-1848
For more information about the history of California

INDEX

Bye, Golden State.
We had a great time.
We'll come back soon!